This is a story about
a cute little
monkey named Lucy.

Lucy is a capuchin monkey that
loves, loves, loves …

Lucy loves bananas,
Bananas are her thing.

When Lucy gets a big banana it always makes her sing.

She loves bananas so very much, she has about five a day

She does not like them limp

Lucy loves bananas, and this is what she do

She does not like them short or soft, she likes them hard and long

Lucy loves bananas,
Bananas are everywhere

Made in United States
Orlando, FL
07 February 2025